Thin Ice

SHEILA LARGE

MOSAÏQUEPRESS

First published in 2019

MOSAÏQUE PRESS
Registered office:
70 Priory Road
Kenilworth, Warwickshire
CV8 1LQ

ISBN 978-1-906852-49-8

Some say the world will end in fire,
Some say in ice.
From what I've tasted of desire.
I hold with those who favor fire.
But if it had to perish twice
I think I know enough of hate
To say that for destruction ice
Is also great
And would suffice.

   – *Robert Frost*

Contents

Winds of change

I set about my eco house with gusto.
A rising helix of straw bales beneath
five oscillating wind sails. Ingenious.

My sister was more gung-ho
when she got the bug. A rustic chalet
with log walls. Deep in the woods. Snug.

He had to go one better. Big bro.
With his massive redbrick pile. Soaring turrets,
the odd twisted spire. Sheer arrogance over style.

Indestructible. He boasted. Smug sod.
One night the weather turned with dire
consequences. A hurricane howled round

the full moon. The log cabin soon became
a nubble of firewood. The top-heavy towers
did for the faux chateau. Razed to rubble.

My straw house took flight. A whirling
quinquereme. Landed right side up.
Unscathed. By a babbling mountain stream.

Tell the truth I'm glad of the excuse
to get out of that place. Apart from the awful weather,
rumour is there's a ferocious wolf on the loose.

Our discreditable secret
from Dylan to Caitlin Thomas

Easier perhaps if we never had met
Nor loved at all; just blessed oblivion.
Our maelstrom versus eternal regret.

He pawned your soul then reneged
on the debt. Devil. Defiler. Rapist.
Rapscallion.

Gorged on you like a stalking great egret.
Devouring all as cast-off carrion.

I too defiled you. My bethralled marionette
Trapped you by your clipped-feather pinion.
Hopeless debaucher & sottish coquette.
Mistimed bells in a fool-struck carillon.

Rage on through the night.
I'm beyond your worst threat.
I deserted too soon.
Yes, death has dominion.

Our maelstrom versus eternal regret
Love has no choice, no defining criterion.
Yet easier perhaps if we never had met.

Summer elsewhere

after Michael Roberts (1902-1948) Hymn to the Sun

'*Fait chaud*', say the old women, toiling
up the hill as the sun reaches its summit.
A near-blind dog chasing lizards around

their slow, determined feet. The heat hangs
heavy and still. Where the beech trees meet
overhead, they share a kiss. Reminisce

how once they had cycled the hill in five minutes.
Now they sit. Quiescent, as befits, short years
off their century. Wasps buzz lazily.

The air pulsates. An old lime dozes. Tang
of citrus fills the air. Next door fires up
her wheezing *voiturette*. Rarely used.

Drives off in a cloud of dust. Wearing
her best hat. Simple lives holding quiet
secrets like sifting sand. Red geraniums

nod against a china-blue sky. The Angelus
bell still ordains the time. Memory remains.
In this enduring paradigm of summer.

Avoid clichés – like the plague

On the advice of a friend I tried killing
two small birds with one stone. The resulting
mess was appalling. It turned me vegetarian.

'Leave no turn unstoned,' said our teacher,
embarrassingly getting it wrong wrong. But then
it was the sixties. Maybe the dope was too strong.

Although I watched pennies for hours
the lonely pound in my pocket, flatly
refused to look after itself. It said
it just couldn't hack it. I once had

a gypsy boyfriend. He was strangely
middle of the road. So I dumped him for the
man in the street, who of course was an

absolute toad. He wove a tangled web of deceit.
Lies I could never impeach. But as my mother said
when he left me, 'There's plenty more fish

on the beach.' Don't go following rainbows
now that's really sound advice. Better to come with me
skating. Look here's some really thin ice.

Careless delight

You came to me in careless delight,
hiding behind your smiling mask, lies
lies and lies and lies and lies,
All your faithless reasoning.

Relief like beads of intimate sweat,
breaking out on your fickle face
face and face and face and face,
up to how much I'm hurting.

In huge great crashing waves of ache
and tiny flaying lashes that sting
sting and sting and sting and sting,
to make sure I'm still remembering.

Closing my eyes to shut out tears
like shards of sharpened ice that cut
cut and cut and cut and cut,
me until it's ice I'm crying.

But you won't see my dry-ice tears.
This will be my secret forever
forever and ever and ever and ever
stubbornly defying

you to ever see what you did to me
when your careless delight was over
over and over and over and over
again and again and again and again,
my stupid heart denying –
you came to me in careless delight.

Dressed to kill

She does not intend, Madame Le Tanneur
metaphorically stamps her dainty foot,

to go to the Mayor's ball again in leather. Sick
to death of it she is. Can't stand the sight. The touch.

The truly terrible stink. Madame Le Tanneur wrinkles
her little retroussé nose. She wants so much

to be chic. Elegant. Wear finest silk. With
a pochette of snakeskin and a stole of mink.

Monseiur Le Tanneur goes out hunting.
Comes across a grand hare, languishing

by the roadside. Dignified. Impeccable in his
autumn-hued coat. He looks very fine

for a short while. Along strides a great tortoise.
Stepping leisurely. Head held high.

Intelligent. Proud. He too is soon naked.
And in his case, also homeless.

Escorting his wife to the ball, Monsieur Le Tanneur
is all too aware of the scrawny russet stole around

her slender neck. The crude carapace purse
at her mincing wrist. He thinks of the dapper hare,

so poised. The sage old tortoise with his stately strut.
They had portrayed elegance indeed.

His wife displays anything but.

Spaghetti Scrabble

You offered a romantic spaghetti,
I should have known it would come
from a tin. Less amore more alphabetti.

Nervously arranging the pieces of pasta,
in tomato sauce like some bloody disaster,
you didn't even try to see what those letters
meant to me. Oh this was your lexicon
to be certain.

Take. Fake. Headache.
Late. Berate. Procrastinate.

Mine told a different story.
Solidarity. Synchronicity. Serendipity,
Warm and storm. Together all too seldom.

Thought I saw heart with sweet
and ache and burn and break
but it was heat. The R lost.
Heart-broken.

There was an O a V and an E,
desperately hoping to start with an L.
Instead it says OVER.
That lost R at the end.
Damn you.
You could never spell.

Chucked

The cold in the park was ferocious.
A dismal mist crept around my
heart. Fearful. Hopeless.

Like the alcoholics. Turned out
of the shelter. Breath frozen and
intoxicating, they mime to cadge fags.
Arms and lives out of kilter.

Leaves whirl. 'Useless leave blowers,'
you say, 'a rake would do as well.
But I rather enjoy the swirling
dervish the manic leaves make.

Playing for time. In my head I make
rhymes. You depend. It must end.

It's been ten years since that
cold winter day. Yet I don't think
I'll ever forget. How I gave you
the ultimatum. And you
smoked your last cigarette.

A cry from the heart

I hear the mindless, screeching cries come
and go. As I struggle with the tiny pleats
on a fine silk chemise. Hysterical whoops float

down from the ridiculous Big Wheel. Smart
carriages. All mahogany and brass. First
and second class. My poor weak heart flips over

at the sight. The height! Forty years I've laundered
for the best of Paris. And that silly *belle-fille*
of mine suggests we modernise. Electricity,

she says, is the thing. Invest. Times are changing.
I told my son. Never. She should get her foolish
head out of the clouds. And as though to mock me

she takes a whole day off. Liberated from the
the steaming heat. The cumbrous irons. High
over the sweltering streets. Screeching.

Barefoot princess

on the launch of £3,000 designer crystal shoes

Every girl wants a Prince Charming,
is an assumption beyond the pale.
And glass footwear is more than alarming,
it belongs in a fairy tale.

It's an assumption beyond the pale
Cinderella, toes in the cinders
it belongs in a fairy tale.
All she wanted was cosy slippers.

Cinderella, toes in the cinders,
a rag doll forced into riches.
All she wanted was cosy slippers
and rid of those two bitches.

A rag doll forced into riches
with a fancy coach drawn by vermin.
She just wanted rid of those bitches
and slippers fashioned from ermine.

With a golden coach drawn by vermin,
who needs some flashy Prince Charming.
She'd rather have slippers of ermine –
glass footwear is more than alarming.

The Peace

We grew up on the north side of a lamp-black
lake in the *Auberge de la Paix*. That knew little
of peace. Or comfort. As my father raged over

the reservoir at his *bête noire*, M. Heureaux,
patron of the *Hôtel de Charme*. Basking
in sunlight. Windows winking above boxes

of pink pelargoniums. Jasmine twined. Wisteria
adorned. A rakish moustache of blonde beach
curved beneath warm, ochre stone. The ancient

doors invite. Visitors flock. While our crenellated
Gothic horror broods. Gardens sulk. Roses shrivel.
Unkempt lavender, violet as a bruise, skirts

the once-white rendered walls, where black mould
blossoms. The vicious *polémique* over fishing rights
endures conflagration and occupation. Provides

the perfect excuse for insults. '*Collaborateur,*'
each side would mutter. Dishonestly. But history
moves on. Weather alters. Summers blister.

Fish expire. Rains lash. Flash floods rise high.
Higher. Heureaux sandbags his doors. Fears
for his window boxes. His treasured beach

long gone. On our decrepit terrace my father
bides. Scans the fragile dam for signs of breach.
Raises a defiant glass to Heureaux. Against

this unfathomable tide. And across the old divide.

Lighten up

She said she'd been struck by lightning.
Fiery flashes finding secret places.
Igniting a maelstrom of burning desires.

Kissed by a thousand licking flames.
Scorched by smouldering hands of velvet.
Unleashing an inferno of raging fires.

Take care, I said, I know that feeling.
Sorcerers who practise lightning magic,
forked like the tongues of wicked liars,

search far and wide for fallen angels.
Their feathery wings so quick to torch,
especially their own funeral pyres.

That goodnight

from Caitlin to Dylan Thomas

Look at you.
Innocence shining out on a guilty world.
Like you were before the days
life crawled all over you
like an old dog.

Days when the pot boiled cheerily
on the hearth
and words bubbled out like
boiled biscuits.
When the children sat around,
just-scrubbed faces shining.
Holding out clean hands
for bread and dripping.
With a hunger we refused to see.

Then others, when the fish
I caught with my feet, left
their stinking scales all over the table
as they leapt to safety in the pan.
Escaping your sharp knife
and the razor of my tongue.

Nights when I danced by moonlight
across the silver sand.
Held tight your word-dry hand
and took you to safety on the shore.

Or, our courtship ritual. Thumping
your clever head on the bedroom floor.
Though it is their heads I wanted to break
and my own I was banging
against the brick wall of your heart.

Your fluttering, fickle heart. Led
all too easily astray. Now the beat
stops dead in its tracks and
Innocence flies, guiltily, away.

Spare rib

Her voice is celestial music.
Her face Botticelli angelic.
She is innocence. She is promise.
She is Adam's perfect Eve.

Adam's an expert in organic apples.
He lectures on their mystic powers.
He's abroad. Eve is bored,
She reads Soulmates.

Tall, dark, enigmatic. Smoker.
Lightning wit. Very fit.
Offers everlasting fire.

She writes to say she loves firelight.
He replies this surely is fate.
He's called Stanley. Man of mystery.
Eve's intrigued.

Stan is tall, dark, deadly attractive.
His eyes yellow. Compelling. Seductive.
Eve is smitten. Snake-bitten.

Stan wants Eve, he's persuasive.
But Eve is smart. She does crosswords.
She knows that his name
is just one letter away
from Satan.

No going back

Last winter we had to say goodbye.
Hearts that never did quite beat in time,
breaking in perfect harmony.

Returning to our cold lives,
shielding from ourselves,
the warm white light between us.

Springtime. Sap rising.
So wanting an excuse to end celibate Lent
in a feast of unholy lust.
Pent-up passion just waiting to be spent.

Flaming June brought pretty diversion.
A touch of midsummer madness.
Smiles and laughter masking the tears.
Though never replacing the sadness.

It's autumn now. Our first reunion.
Inane exchanges. As the leaves tell their story.
Growing, turning, dying. Inevitable

seasons. The year slipping by.
Never changing the reasons
the sad truth why.
Last winter we had to say goodbye.

Avenging angel

Once through the arch she rests.
Her back warm against the ancient
wall. Her coat jewel-bright against
soft pink stone. Sleek hair glinting silver.
Elegant hand resting on the curved handle
of an ebony stick. Shrill birdsong. Heat
haze shimmering over the distant lake.
Murmur of voices in the background.

Her heels tap slowly as she moves
towards the doors of the *château*.
Crossing weed-strewn paths
of cracked terracotta. Glancing

through the barn door, she half expects
to see his red sports car.
But it has long gone. Along with the *bateau*.
Sold, as it were, down the river.

And today it's the family silver.
The paintings, the pottery, the porcelain,
all once the collection of *grand-père*,
now displayed with the vintage champagne
for sale to the highest bidder.

The public rummages through
the remnants of his life. She
searches with scant delight.
Slow. Laborious.

Then she sees it. Framed
in the panelled hall.
The fresco.

In Florence the old priest had told them
it could be a fragment of work by the Master
this ancient piece of crumbling plaster.
The face of an angel. Beatific. Serene.

He thought it looked like her and bought it.
For more lire than she earned in a year.
Outside Florence seared.

And here it is. Memento of youth,
beauty and pleasure the thrill
of clandestine encounter. Worth more
than her Left Bank apartment. Perhaps.
Or less than its gilded frame.

She leaves her bid and slips quietly away.
With a quiet wish to win. Settle the debt.
The wages of long ago sin.

Later the *château* forms the perfect scene.
A picture postcard in her rear view mirror.
Her face is composed. Beatific. Serene.

The Cathedral

The heat slams like a slap in her face as she
steps out on to the parapet. The city shimmers
to the horizon – impossibly far away. All day

the metro had been her high-speed, rattling
prison. Her inescapable jail. Throat rasped
dry with her own cry. Small brown hands

held out. Her child swaddled tight. Her bright
shawl a cocoon. His fists clutching the tiny
mirrors that festoon the hem. Graffitti mocking

like foreign fog. *Liberté Égalité Fraternité* mean
nothing to her. Freedom and equality are beyond
reach. Brotherhood controls her despair.

It is cooler behind the soaring spire as
she lays her son on unforgiving stone.
Grinning gargoyles beckon hellfire.

The news goes largely unnoticed. An
unregistered *Gitane*. Unequal. Manner of death
uncertain. Case closed. No sequel.

Yet ever after the boy would maintain he could
recall the glow of dying sunlight. Brown ankles
arching. And the flash of tiny mirrors in flight.

Summer storm

It was the sweetest summer madness.
A warm dream to remember by starlight,
when winter's howling round at the moon.

Kisses, smooth like peaches' ripeness,
gentle butterflies trembling bright,
spinning in a sensual cocoon.

Lightning causing temporary blindness,
touch a softer medium than sight.
Rhythm beating in breathless tune.

Busy dawn invading the darkness,
creeping into intimate delight,
stealing precious time too soon.

Shimmering morning; still and flawless,
promising after a stolen night,
the silken rain of a summer monsoon.

The red balloon – Paris 1901

The vast crimson sphere hovers over the dawn-quiet
park below. As high as my grubby attic window.
Filled with hot air - they say. Later today it will rise
above the sweltering streets. And far away
in a village that scarce knows Paris, my sister
will marry. Her beau the childhood foe we taunted and
teased. How easily I see her pretty, nervous face.
The new lace collar on her old dress; above shoulders
that will bear their share of sorrow. Borrowed pearls
pink against her cream skin. Deep blue cornflowers in an old
jug with poppies, bright as grenadine, against the crisp white
cloth. Froth of beer on Papa's moustache. Cigarette ash
dropping. Mama flushed. Brushing it away. Content
for once. Or at least suppressing histrionics. I fix

my austere cap in the cracked mirror. Given me by the
mistress; who has many hours yet to sleep. The sweat
already shows on my coarse dress. I do not weep.
But I offer a silent wish that the startling red balloon
should carry me noiselessly from the stifling aerodrome.
Over goatherd hills and peasant fields. Home.

Faith

On a Tuscan hillside a monk quietly
tends his fruit trees. A passing unbeliever
asks how he feels about wasting his life,

should there be no heaven. He replies
that it is the aethist who is more in danger
of wasting eternity. Five thousand miles

and minus 30 degrees away, Soviet children
are told to close their eyes and ask God
for treats. Naughty Sergei peeps. Just as

the teacher knows he will. Sees her give out
the sweets. Proof that God does not exist. Or
betrayal? The monk's life sounds pretty good.

Content with the scent of lemon flowers. Drifts
of lavender and rosemary. Taste of sun-hot
raspberries in his prayerful mouth. What waste?

Believe me
for Tony Gargan

Martin & Bernard book-end the fire in
their cellar kitchen. Unmarried brothers.
Martin, the thwarted priest, in monochrome.
Platinum hair and marble-white hands
of unusual length. Bernard, sepia survivor
of RMS *Lusitania*. Tobacco-dyed fingers
permanently cupped around a
Capstan Full Strength.

Breaking up for Christmas, heads full
of the Nativity, we children clatter in. Dirty
snowflakes fall outside. Against the red
glow in the black iron grate, a small white
hand descends from the chimney, hovers,
then retracts, slowly, whence it came.
With neither word nor wink from either brother.

Santa's hand. Magical. Incredible. An age-old
family mystery. A bit like the Nativity.

Accidents will

after an idea from Rod Vincent

I never leave mine alone. Not even
for half an hour. Anything might
happen. My brother once electrocuted

himself; messing about with plugs
and the like. Another time my sister
held a candle to my glasses. So

I could appreciate the colours
in the flame. I didn't. Latch-key
kids they called us in those days.

Bloody naughty we were. Mine
are good on the whole. But Daddy
or me are always home. Just in case.

They turn the corner. And there they are.
Good as gold. Holding Daddy's hand.
Next to the fire engine.

Hospital blues

'You're in the wrong place!' She chases
me with a dismissive, Gallic, wave.

In rain-soaked sarong, crutches digging
into every new bruise, I hobble
out again. Lose

a plastic flip-flop in a dirty
puddle that reflects the iron
grey sky. I do not cry.

Afterwards I realise what she, the nurse,
was thinking. Secretly. *Gypsy.*

Then I weep. For inequity.
For myself. For humanity.

Snow melts

On Sunday in snowed.
A clean purity swaddling the familiar
landscape. Transformed. Beautiful

in its silence. Life's mess hidden.
Garden tools left in a heap. Though
I ask you every single day
to put the blessed things away.

Now they form a gentle mound.
A welcome undulation on the
uninteresting, level ground.

Mondays are forever gloomy and today
the snow is gone. Dirty slush fills the streets
and the garden is dull brown once more.

The mound has gone too.
You took the tools with you.

Halloween trick

He practises fantastic magic, holds
precarious fate in both hands. With
dangerous tricks and illusion, his
audience is transfixed. Spellbound.
White doves might appear on his shoulder,
then transform into snakes with a flash.
On a flourish his cane is a dagger, hurled
through the air with panache.

Yet at home his fine wizardry fails him.
Life's decisions too painful to take.
It requires a degree of enchantment.
To help determine his fate. Halloween

draws in misty and mellow. When he knows
he can choose just one option. And
summoning powers of allurement
catches leaves in a trick performed often.
A leaf in each fist – the first open,
red or gold will decide on his plight.

He faces himself in the mirror (knowing
his hands can be sleight). Right and left
each holds a compulsion, though once chosen
his fate will be cast. When he opens his palms
they're both empty,

In delusion his future has passed.

Topical tip

Take one part loam. That's ordinary
garden soil. Not this starved, stony,
French mountain dirt. But rich, black,
salt of the Earth, Muck.

Another of sand. Fine, trickling,
warm to the hand sand. From
a builder's yard, if you must, just
be sure to sieve out
the coarse comments.

Next grit. Well we all need a bit
of that to survive. Any kind of tiny, riven
gravel. The more Northern the better.

Finally, an equal part of composted bark.
Carefully saved from trees that
have given generously of blossom
and fruit. Shade and shelter.

Before falling, content. Ready to take
part in the next big adventure.

Boom

My first was modest, though well-built.
A post-war semi. Half-cut squaddie turned
coach potato. His only ambition
a drinks fridge in the kitchen.

He took the couch. I got the mortgage.
And so made a killing when house prices
soared. Hundred grand in a year, barely time
to get bored. Next came a Victorian relic.

Dodgy plumbing. Infestation. Damp patches.
And that was before he got ill.
His estate was worth several million.
I copped for the lot in his will.

There was an aristocrate with a rich
Texan wife. She gave me a ranch
to get out of his life. There in those Badlands
some sort of amends when I met a
surrealist sculptor.
His installation a perfect wonder.

When his seminal bronze won the next
Turner Prize, I bowed out and bought
half of Scotland. I live in isolated splendour
with a grim tax inspector, who I married
when he got too inquisitive.

I'm a billionaire for sure. I will never
again be poor. But in love,
the equity is negative.

About the author

A poet and writer living in France, Sheila draws on the light and dark for inspiration; both in human relationships and in the natural world. During a diverse career she has published many articles on business, social justice and ecology, while always escaping into poetry and literature. Her influences are American poets from the Twenties to the Fifities, Liverpool poets from the Sixties, Irish and Welsh poets from forever and many contemporary women poets. Her poems have been published in several anthologies and in *Poetry News*. This is her first collection.

www.ingramcontent.com/pod-product-compliance
Lightning Source LLC
Chambersburg PA
CBHW060647030426
42337CB00018B/3493